Trafficked: The Diary of a Sex Slave

Sibel Hodge

My name is Elena and I used to be a human being. Now I am a sex slave. If you are reading this diary then I am either dead or I have managed to escape...

Day 1

For the first time since I was a little child, I am lost. I have no idea where I am, although I have not travelled far, so I must still be in Moldova. I remember getting lost at a busy market when I was about four years old. My mother turned away to haggle over vegetables with a stall holder, and I wandered off at the lure of something bright-coloured and pretty in the distance. In a sea of legs, I disappeared, and when I turned to look for my mother again, I could not find her. I screamed, of course, crying out for her. When eventually we were reunited, I hugged her tight and would not let her go. I followed her around for weeks afterwards so the same thing never happened again.

Now I am lost and my mother cannot help me. No amount of crying or screaming will get me out of here. I have tried.

I know what is going on. I have heard the stories from nearby villages but I never thought it could happen to me. You don't, do you?

Trust. It is such a small word but it can have such a big effect on your life.

I trusted my best friend when she told me her boyfriend could get us both a job in a casino in Italy. I had no reason not to trust her. We have been friends since we could talk. In all this time I never thought she would betray me. Am I naïve or just stupid? I have a feeling I will wonder this a lot in the coming days.

There is nothing else to do at the moment but sit and think of a way out of here. Somehow, I fear it will be impossible, though. I have decided to keep this diary in case I never get out. It is hidden in my rucksack, in a gap underneath the lining at the bottom. If they find it, I will be in serious trouble. Maybe writing it will stop me going mad, and hopefully my family will eventually know what happened to me.

I can picture my mother's wrinkled face and see my daughter Liliana's gappy-toothed smile. Liliana is four years old, and she is my life. I need to survive for her, but they have told me if I try to escape, they will kill her and my mother. I have seen the cold hatred in their eyes as they described to me in detail exactly what they would do to them, and I know they would not hesitate to carry out their threats.

I should explain how I came to be locked in this small bedroom somewhere in Moldova, because I need you to know that none of this is my fault.

I am twenty-two years old and live in a poor village. Most people are living hand-to-mouth – maybe on less than a dollar a day. Moldova has a very high rate of unemployment, and they say it is one of the poorest countries in Europe. People in our village sold their kidneys on the black market just to keep them in food. They could make around $500 for one kidney. You can do the maths

2

to know that is a fortune. I wonder how much the rate is for a sex slave.

Some people have sold their children to the slave gangs, too. I heard of one woman whose husband died. She had seven children she could not afford to feed anymore so she sold three of her daughters to the sex mafia. I always wondered what happened to her girls. Maybe they are here, in this place, and I will see them again.

How could she do that to her children? Her daughters would be better off dead than suffering what they must have to endure. If they are alive, they are surely in a living hell. I think of Liliana's innocent face, the way she cuddles up to me for a story. She trusts me. How could I ever put her in danger? To save my other children? Is that a good enough reason?

Natalia, my so-called best friend, told me her boyfriend Andrei knew of some jobs working in a casino in Italy where the wages were €500 a month. A month! Imagine so much money. Natalia said the casino would even pay our travelling fare.

I had it all figured out. Liliana could stay with my mother for a month, just until I got everything arranged in Italy. I would find a small apartment using my wages and bring them both to live with me. It would be perfect. A way out of this country to a world of new opportunities.

It was a very emotional goodbye with Liliana and my mother. Liliana held onto my legs and did not want to let go. We all cried so much. I promised them as soon as I got an apartment I would send for them and we would be together again. It would not be long, a month at the most.

I arranged to meet Natalia at the bus station in town. We were going to be picked up by a friend of Andrei who would drive us all the way to Italy. But when I found Natalia she told me there was a problem with her passport and she would not be able to go until it was sorted out. She talked me into going without her.

'It will only be a week or so before I join you,' she said. 'Don't worry, Andrei and his friend will look after you.' She smiled and hugged me.

And I trusted her.

Andrei's friend did not drive me to Italy. I am still somewhere in Moldova. I was blindfolded and handcuffed and threatened with death in the car before I arrived here with my captor. If I did not do what they ordered, they told me they would do unspeakable things to Liliana and my mother before they kill them. I cannot risk their lives so I must do what they tell me.

I am in a house, I think, in the country. There are no city noises here, only birds chirping. I never thought I would envy a bird, but I do. They are free to fly away from here, and I imagine I am a sparrow or an owl, launching myself through the windows to freedom. But there are bars on the windows and the shutters are closed, so there is no way for me to escape. I have tried the door but it is locked with a key and bolted from the outside. It is dark in my prison cell, and I think I have been here for about eight hours so it must be night time by now. I am in a whitewashed room about two metres square, and I am lying on an old mattress that smells of urine and filth, with my hands and feet in chains. There is a bucket in here for me to go to the toilet. No paper to use, though, and the thought of being unable to wipe myself disgusts me.

There are other girls here, too. I can hear them through the walls, crying and screaming. I want to talk to them; to get some comfort from knowing we are together, but I do not dare. If my captors hear me talking it may make them angry. Earlier I heard a door burst open nearby and a man's voice yelling at one of the girls to be quiet. I heard slaps and punches, and her high-pitched screams that pierced my brain, even though my hands were pressed tightly over my ears. Now I hear just her soft sobs.

I know what happened; I could hear that, too.

Day 2

One of my captors is a woman. It is unbelievable to think that a woman could be involved in something like this. Women are mothers and nurturers. How can she do this to another woman, knowing what will happen to us? Somehow that makes her worse than the men. Does living in poverty and the sudden prospect of money make people evil, or are they evil to begin with?

I begged for a toilet roll and she gave me one. I know from now on it is the little things that I took for granted in life that will make me feel like a human being again. Toilet roll – an everyday item, and yet I am so happy to see it.

It is morning, I think. She unlocked the door and left a plate of bread and salted dried fish. She gave me a big bottle of water, too. My thirst seemed to have come from nowhere, and I forgot that I had had nothing to eat or drink for twenty-four hours. I swallowed half the bottle without stopping for air. I cannot eat, though. My stomach is churning at the thought of things to come.

I wanted to ask how she could do this to us, but I cannot antagonize her. She is a hard-looking woman, about thirty-five years old. She has nice hair and make-up, and her clothes are expensive. I hear her laughing and joking with the male captors like this is all perfectly normal. In her world I suppose it is.

Instead, I asked her what was going to happen to me, and she told me I am now owned by a slave gang. Soon they will transport me and the other girls across Europe to Italy. She said they have my passport and I must do as they say. She told me how they had killed other girls' family members when they disobeyed them. I do not want to listen to her, but I have to. The seventy-five-year-old mother of one of the girls who tried to escape was strung up from a tree and hanged. The seven-year-old daughter of one of the girls who tried to escape was tortured. She had all her nails and teeth pulled out with pliers before being stabbed a hundred times. On and on she went, telling me horrific things like that.

I forced the bile down in my throat and willed the tears not to fall. I cannot show weakness, they will try to use it against me.

As she left the room, she smirked at me. 'Night night,' she said, even though it must be daytime.

As I drain the last of the water, I finally know what she meant. I am feeling very sleepy now and must hide my diary.

I think they have drugged me.

Day 4

There will be some days when I cannot write in here. Yesterday was one of those days. I woke up in a van with six other girls. There were two men in the front of the van, and Andrei's friend was driving. I recognized one of the men's voices. He was the one who raped the crying girl in the room near mine. The Rapist has a shaved head and a big, bulky body. He has blue eyes that seem to stare right through you, and his teeth are wonky and stained. The second man is taller and even bigger than the Rapist. He puffed on a cigarette continuously and chatted to the others friends about football and gambling.

I was still dopey when we came to the border with Romania, but I tried to force myself awake. I glanced at girls around me who were still asleep. I thought that surely the immigration guards would know something was wrong and stop us. Wouldn't they find the van suspicious? Wouldn't they rescue us? I wanted to be alert so when they arrested the gang of men, I would be able to get home to my mother and Liliana as quickly as possible.

As we drew along side the immigration booth a guard got out and spoke to Andrei's friend through the driver's window. The Rapist handed a collection of passports to the guard, who barely flicked through them before peering into the small window at the back of the van where I was sitting. For a second my eyes connected with his, and I could see a brief flicker of sadness and pity etched into his face. At that moment I knew he knew what was happening to us. I held his gaze, tempted to mouth the words, "Help me". Then he quickly turned away from me and waved the truck on, and I knew it would have done no good anyway. You cannot transport so many girls a year from Moldova to other countries to be sex slaves without the border guards or people high up knowing about it. I wondered how they would feel if it happened to their daughters or sisters or wives. Would they feel the same then?

I rested my head against the window, staring out at the endless road ahead for what felt like half a day. Some of the other girls had started to wake up by now and it was the first time we got to look into each other's eyes. I know my own desperation and dread must have been mirrored in theirs, and I could smell the fear on their bodies. I wanted to ask them who they were. Who had they trusted that got them in this situation? What was their story? But none of us spoke. To speak meant it was real.

Andrei's friend pulled the van over at the side of the road and gave us all more water laced with drugs, forcing us to drink it. I did not want to drink it, but what choice did I have? I knew when I woke up things would be worse.

Soon after the liquid entered my system I felt sleep threatening to overtake me again. I closed my eyes and imagined myself with Liliana, my arms around her fragile body and my lips resting on top of her head. I could almost smell her shampoo.

Her face was the last thing I saw before I sunk into darkness.

The next time I woke up it felt like I was trapped in some kind of box. I could not turn around; the space was too small, like a coffin, and dark. My throat felt dry and scratchy, and my muscles were stiff. I tried to swallow, but I had no moisture in my mouth. My head pounded with the worst headache I had ever experienced, and I felt nauseous, my stomach bubbling away. I had not eaten for a long time so I had no food to bring up. Instead, I felt acid bile in my throat. I sucked my tongue to stimulate some saliva so I could swallow, and this seemed to help. I could hear the hum of traffic speeding past, horns occasionally blaring out, and the steady bump, bump, bump of the road.

I slept and woke many times during the drive. Thoughts of what happened to the other girls drifted into my head. Had they been killed? Would I be killed? Were the other girls the lucky ones who managed to escape somehow?

I had no concept of time, but it felt like days until I was shaken from sleep by the Rapist. He opened the lid to my coffin, which was hidden in the floor of a van, and yanked me out by my arm. My whole body was stiff, and trying to make it work took some effort. I stumbled as he dragged me out of the van into the dark night. We were parked outside a big house in a residential area.

I could smell his bad breath as he gripped my arm and pulled me around the back of the house. The Rapist opened the back door and pushed me into a kitchen where a big man with a beard who was watching TV nodded and said hello to the Rapist. The lights burned my eyes at first until they adjusted to the brightness, but I could see the bearded man grin leeringly at me.

'Here is the new girl,' the Rapist said to a woman wearing a short black dress, high heels, and red lipstick who was playing cards with the bearded man. She was not much older than me; maybe twenty-five. She slowly took a puff on her cigarette and studied me carefully.

'Very pretty.' She stubbed out the cigarette in an overflowing ashtray and walked towards me as the Rapist still gripped my arm. 'Do you know how to use a condom?' she asked, as casually as if she were asking about the weather.

My stomach lurched as I imagined what was to come.

The Rapist twisted my arm behind my back, yanking it upwards. 'Answer her.'

I yelped and nodded at the woman.

'Good.' She smiled with satisfaction then grabbed my chin in her hands and turned my face this way and that to get a better look at me. 'She is an excellent find. The men will love her,' she said to the Rapist.

'I do not want to sleep with any men,' I whispered. '*Please,* I'll do anything else you want. I will cook or clean or–'

The Rapist tugged on my arm again so hard I thought my shoulder would pop out of its socket. 'You will do as we say. We own you now. I think it is time I taught you a lesson.'

He dragged me out of the kitchen by my hair, and through a living room where there were several women wearing hardly any clothes. The only thing I noticed as they stared at me stumbling past was their eyes looked dead.

I screamed as he pulled me up some stairs towards the top of the house. He pushed open a doorway with a lock on the outside, and into a bedroom. He punched me in the stomach and I doubled over as the wind disappeared from my lungs.

He let out a cackling laugh, and I could smell his dirty breath in the air. He banged my head into the metal bedpost and I fell to the floor, struggling to breathe. And then everything happened so fast it is hard to remember which order it happened.

He pulled my hair, slapped me, kicked me, punched me, pinched me. I tried to bring my arms up to my head to protect myself by curling into a ball, but then he was on top of me. He grabbed my arms and held them above my head with one hand as he ripped off my skirt and knickers with the other. Then he forced my legs apart with his knee and he was inside me.

In my head I screamed, "No, no, no," over and over again, but nothing came out of my mouth. I screwed my eyes shut and tried to think of something else, but the pain everywhere kept me from concentrating.

'You're a fucking whore, and you will do what I tell you,' he shouted in my ear.

I could hear myself whimpering but it sounded like it was coming from someone else far off in the distance; like I was disconnected from my body.

After a final thrust, he lifted his heavy body off mine and zipped up his trousers. I finally got my wish and curled in a foetal position on the floor to try and stop the pain. I could not hold back the tears anymore. They streamed down my face, stinging the grazes, but I did not care anymore if he saw my weakness.

With a kick to my back he towered over me and laughed. 'Do you get it now?' he said. 'If you do not want that to happen to your daughter, you will do everything we say.' Then he spat in my face, left the room, and locked the door behind him.

This is now my life.

Day 7

I could not bring myself to write anything for the last few days. Everywhere hurts, even my hands. I have cried so much that I do not think I have any water left in my body.

I have never believed in God but I find myself praying. I am not sure who to, but I feel like I have to. If there is a God, how could He let this happen? I do not believe there is any kind of higher being who can help me now. My prayers are not to any kind of God, they are silent messages to keep me strong.

Thoughts of Liliana and my mother fill my mind. I wish I could talk to them and tell them I miss them so much there is an ache squeezing my heart. I want to hear their voices and hold them tight. I want to wake up from this nightmare and be safe in their arms.

I think of my father and my husband Stefan, too. They have been dead several years, and for once, I am glad. It would rip them apart to know what has happened to me.

I was lucky in one way, growing up, because my father was a skilled man. If anything broke down he could usually fix it himself. He seemed to have a natural gift of understanding how things worked, and people from the surrounding villages would always call on him to repair things. Because of this, we were better off than a lot of our neighbours, and when he died, he left my mother some small savings. Things have still not been easy for us, but it helped until the money ran out and I needed desperately to get a job.

My father taught me English when I was young. I do not know where he got the books from, but somehow he could find anything he wanted – he was a very resourceful man. He knew the only way to better myself was to learn English and seek new opportunities in another country. He wanted me to do something special with my life – it was his dream to see it happen.

And maybe it would have happened if he and Stefan had not both been killed in a car accident the day I found out I was pregnant with Liliana.

I cannot change the past, and now I have no control over the future, either. It is ironic that I finally made it to another country, but it will not be to better myself.

Day 8

The woman I met with the red lipstick has been quite kind to me. Her name is Angelina and she runs this brothel. She is the girlfriend of the leader of this Italian gang who bought me. I have learned I am in Milan, but I doubt I will ever see anything of this city. I have been locked in my room since I arrived. Having seen the other girls with the dead eyes in the lounge, I think it is yet another form of punishment for me to stay in here.

Lying on the double bed, aching, I have had the chance to study my bedroom in great detail. There is nothing else for me to do that will keep my mind active, other than write in my diary.

My room is clean and bright, painted in a pale yellow with cream curtains that are frayed slightly at the edges and have a smudged stain at the top. I have a small toilet, sink, and shower in an en suite bathroom, for which I am grateful. Somehow, it makes it seem a little less like a prison cell. The second tile on the floor as you enter the bathroom has a chip on it in the shape of a star. The ceiling has an old cobweb in the far corner, dangling in the breeze. I can gaze out of the window and, through the bars, I see the cloudless blue sky, sunshine, and tops of the houses. I can hear the sounds of a busy city echoing around me – people going about their life as if everything in the world is normal.

Angelina brings me food and water, which is very basic and bland: bread, pasta, cereal, cucumbers. I long for the sweet biscuits I used to have for breakfast, and tasty meat goulash my mother makes. I can almost smell it as I wonder what is happening at home.

Every night the Rapist comes and forces himself on me. He said it is good practice for me. He is trying to break me in and make me a willing slave. He does not want to beat me anymore because he wants me to look pretty, but he told me he will if he has to. When my bruises have gone they will expect me to sleep with the men who come here. From 10 p.m. to 10 a.m. every night I must do what these men want. If I am good and cause no problems, he said nothing will happen to Liliana and my mother.

Angelina thinks I should be grateful her boyfriend bought me. There are much worse places for a girl to end up, she told me, and described shabby brothels and dirty saunas in town who buy girls.

'They are seedier than here,' she said. 'They are filthy places, and the men are often drunk and they stink. They go there after working in factories or on farms and do not bother to wash beforehand. At least here the men are clean and have more manners.' She waved her hand around the room. 'This is one of the nicest brothels in Milan. And when you are not working you can use the lounge and kitchen space, but you cannot leave the house.

There are guards here at all times. If you are good, you can stay here. If not,' she shrugged her shoulders, as if the choice in the matter really was mine alone, 'you will go to those other places.'

Maybe I should be grateful that I am here and not in one of the places she described, but I cannot summon that emotion from anywhere within.

She gave me lacy underwear, thongs, French knickers, bras, crotchless knickers, stockings and suspenders. I must wear only underwear when the men come to choose the girls.

I cannot look at these items. I do not want them on my body. I do not want this.

Day 9

I have never hated anyone in my life, but I hate Natalia, and I hate the Rapist. I hate the way he forces himself on me. I hate the pain he causes my insides. I hate his chilling blue eyes and his stale breath. I hate the sex.

My bruises are fading now and can be covered with make-up. Angelina has told me that tonight I must work. She told me she can give me drugs to relax me if I want. I do not know whether that is a good or bad thing. Part of me wants to be out of it; not to know what is really happening to my body, but I think that once they control you with drugs you will never get away, even if you want to.

She brushed my waist-length black hair until it was silky and told me how to wear it. She showed me how to do my make-up so I look "sexy." She picked out which underwear to put on.

My stomach is in knots. I cannot eat anything as the minutes of the day tick by. All I can think about is what will happen to me. What will these men expect? How many will there be? Will they give me a disease? How much pain will it cause? Will they beat me? How can I get through this and still be a fully functioning person?

My mind will be raped as well as my body. I am no longer me anymore but a skeleton of the woman I was.

But I must do it for Liliana and my mother. I must act the part. I will become an Oscar winning actress, because one day I will get out of here. I do not know how long it will take, but I cannot allow myself to believe that I will never get away, because if I do believe that, then I may as well kill myself now.

I could do it easily. I could break the mirror on the dressing table and slit my wrists or my throat. I could take a knife from the kitchen and do it. I could save up all the drugs they offer me and take them all at once. I have thought about it, of course I have, but what if they take revenge on my family? I could not be responsible for that.

So I need to believe there is hope for me, even if it is just a tiny strand in the midst of all this pain. Without hope I will not survive this.

Day 10

I used to be a human being, but now I am a sex slave. I will never be clean again. No matter how many times I scrub and scrub, trying to claw off my skin, I will always have their dirt everywhere. On my skin, under my nails, inside me, and etched into my soul.

Last night the girls with dead eyes waited for men in the lounge. When the men came, they chose which slave they wanted, and the girls led them to their rooms in silence.

When I was a little girl I saw a cow being mated, and its haunting cries stayed with me all this time. It was tied in a narrow metal pen so it could not move, and they brought a bull in the pen behind to have sex with it. The cow's eyes rolled in its head and it made a desperate noise, as if it wanted to escape.

Sex with these men is the same. I am trapped and I am at their mercy. I could not cry like the cow so I stayed silent, but my eyes were closed and I went to another place. I wanted to scream, "No!" but I could not. Behind my eyelids I pictured Liliana, safe with my mother, playing with her favourite soft toy, a dog called Ivan. Ivan is saggy and worn now from years of use. He has one eye missing and his right ear is half falling off, in need of stitching.

Liliana talked to me. She told me she is safe and warm and loved. She misses me and wants me to come home, and when she said this, a silent tear snaked down my cheek. The men did not notice this. They are on top of me, behind me, below me, inside me, but they do not really see me. I am a thing, a toy, an object. A slave who is there purely for them to release their fantasies.

In my daydream about Liliana she was doing well with her reading. My mother had taught her to read a new book. Liliana is bright and learns quickly. She devours stories, and one day I hope she will be a doctor or a lawyer. She had a dusting of sugar around her mouth from eating too many sweet biscuits my mother loves to make.

Ten men had sex with me last night. Part of me feels such strong emotions, and part of me feels like it has died. I am grieving for the part of me that I will never get back. I am ashamed, guilty, disgusted. I feel hatred and anger, but I cannot let that show. I had to pretend I enjoyed it, but it made me feel sick. Physically sick to my core. And there is a part of me that feels numb because I do not want to think of what has happened to me. What *is* happing to me. It seems like I have become a ghost, trapped in a twenty-two year old body, looking out at the world. But no one sees me.

And when I think about Stefan, I know our lovemaking was real. It was gentle and unselfish. I try not to think about that because I miss him too much. And I know I will never be normal again. I will never think about a lover in the same way as I did with Stefan. My scars will not show, but they will torture me forever.

Why did this happen to me? To the other girls? Doesn't anyone else know what is going on in the world? Why don't they send someone to help us?

I feel sorry for all the bad things I have done in my life, but I will never believe that this is my fault. I never asked for this, I just wanted to give my family a better life.

Now, when I look in the mirror, I have dead eyes, too.

Day 15

I have not written much because I do not want to describe the things they make me do. You can imagine every depravity and increase it a hundred times, then you will understand.

I try to take comfort in the daylight hours. The girls are allowed out of their rooms, and we can watch TV and make food for ourselves when we are not working. I do not eat much and can see my ribs and hip bones jutting through my skin. My cheeks are gaunt and my hair is dull and lifeless. Every few hours I think about killing myself. Maybe I would be better off dead. But then I think of Liliana and know I can never do it.

Most of the girls do not talk about where they are from or who they used to be before they were stolen.

I trust no one now. How do I know they would not repeat what I say to Angelina or the Rapist?

I do hang around with one girl called Sasha who is from Russia. I never speak about my own situation, but we spend time in each other's rooms, and she told me how she was trafficked from her small village three years ago. She was living with her mother when two men came late at night and banged on the door. Her mother was working a night shift at a chicken factory so she was not there to try and protect her. When Sasha opened the door, the men knocked her unconscious, and when she woke up, she was in an apartment somewhere. She stayed there for a week as the men and his friends took turns with her. They sold her to a trader in England, and she was forced to work on the street or in massage parlours. Recently she was sold to a sauna, where she was locked in her room twenty-four hours a day. The men who came and had sex with her every night would often be drunk and beat her. The sauna charged £50 per customer, but she never received any money. She tried to tell some of the men what happened to her so they would take pity on her and get her out. None of them did. They did not care how she got there. When she refused to do things for the men, the brothel owner beat her up. Half her hair was pulled out and she had broken fingers and toes where he stamped on them. He broke a rib, as well, that hasn't healed properly and sticks out at a strange angle. Sometimes she has trouble breathing. As she described this I could actually hear the crunching of bone in her words. She took off the wig she wears and showed me how her hair has not yet grown back properly.

After the beating she was sold to Angelina's boyfriend and arrived here. In the last three years she has been sold eight times, but she said this is the nicest brothel she has been imprisoned in.

Do I take comfort in that? It is strange but part of me does. There are worse places I could end up.

She told me of another girl she met in England who was also from Moldova. She managed to escape and went to the Moldovan embassy who arranged for her to return to her home, but when she arrived, she discovered she was pregnant. The gang that originally trafficked her tracked her down, raped and beat her so she lost her baby. They killed her family's pet dog as an extra punishment and threatened to kill her family if she escaped again. She was then re-trafficked back to England. Some of the girls Sasha knew have gone missing suddenly and she thinks they have been murdered.

Sasha wanted to tell me more but I stopped her. That was enough for me to hear for one day. I want to know because it might help me save myself. I want to know what makes people do this to us. I want to know how these things can happen in the twenty-first century. I want to know if I can ever find a way to escape.

Day 20

Last night the police arrived. It was after midnight and I was waiting in the lounge for yet another man to take me. Sasha was there, too, along with six other girls.

When I saw two policemen arrive in uniform with their guns strapped at their sides I thought the house was being raided. For the first time in weeks I had real hope. They would get us out of here and send me back to Moldova. Soon I would have my arms wrapped so tight around Liliana that I would never let go again. These men were going to save us!

Maybe I was wrong about God. Could he have heard my prayers for help?

I felt breathless with excitement, and I had to hold onto a table to steady my legs and stop me collapsing with relief.

'Oh, thank you,' escaped from my mouth before I knew I was speaking. My hands flew to my cheeks as I smiled and waited for them to get us out of there. 'Thank you for helping us,' I said to the policemen.

Sasha shook her head at me, giving me a silent warning that these men were not our saviours.

The older policeman in the group glanced up at me with mild amusement, and I could see from the look on his face they were not there to help us.

Suddenly I could barely breathe. My heart beat erratically, pumping hard and out of time. A crushing pain squeezed my chest and I fainted.

When I woke up I was in my bedroom. The older policemen was thrusting inside me, his coffee breath suffocating me. Then the other policeman took his turn with me. And when they were finished, the Rapist came to teach me a lesson.

Day 23

I am burning up. My body feels like it is constantly on fire, and yet I am as cold as ice. I have been in bed for three days, unable to move. Sometimes I see Liliana at my bedside. She is holding some hand-picked flowers out to me.

'Get well soon, Mummy,' she says.

I reach out for her, but she is too far away. Then I drift into nothingness again.

Day 25

A doctor was here. I do not know what kind of doctor he is. I thought doctors took an oath to heal their patients. How can he know I am here and just leave me with these people?

He said I have a severe urine and kidney infection, and has given me strong antibiotics. I feel sore inside my vagina, and I know something is not right there, too.

He examined me internally and I flinched at his touch. Yet another unwanted man on my skin.

'You have tears inside,' he said. 'In a few days they will heal.'

But what about my heart? Will that heal? I wanted to ask.

I feel like I am dying – burning up from the inside out. I cannot move from my bed, I am too weak, so the doctor has inserted a catheter inside me.

I do not know how much more I can take.

Angelina brought me some chicken soup and bread. She told me they will lose money because I cannot work for a while. Her boyfriend is not happy with me.

'If you try anything like this again, we will sell you to somewhere much worse,' she said.

I wanted to scream and cry and yell, and tell her it is not me! It is you, it is your boyfriend, it is the

Rapist, it is the policemen. They are the ones who have done bad things, not me. This is not my fault.

Of course, I cannot say that. I just nodded at her so she knew I understood.

When she left I fantasized about escaping. Maybe there is a chance the policemen can help me after all. They just do not know it yet.

Day 26

Sasha keeps me company. She brushes my hair and sings to me. It reminds me of how I used to put Liliana's hair in bunches and pigtails, making up silly songs to keep her still until I had finished.

I am strong enough to get out of bed for short periods but I do not want to. Sasha sits on my bed and plays cards with me, even though I do not want to talk to anyone. I would rather keep the covers over my head in a darkened cocoon and cry, but Sasha will not take no for an answer.

I think she knows what I am thinking. She chewed on her bottom lip, waiting for me to talk. I did not tell her anything. I would like to think I can trust her, but how do I really know for sure? I cannot tell my plan to anyone.

I need to know what happened to the girls she met in the last three years. I want to ask her outright if any of them escaped forever. Did any of them get their freedom permanently, or were they always dragged back to this life by their pimps and traders? If I ask her that she will know for certain what I am thinking. So instead, I just asked her to talk to me as I lay with my eyes closed. Her voice is soothing, and it did not take long before she was telling me about her life in Russia.

Like me, Sasha thinks about what is happening at home. She said her mother must believe she is dead, and she cannot bear this thought sometimes.

I know how she feels. Liliana and my mother will be frantic with worry that they have not heard from me. I promised to get word to them when I arrived safely in Italy. By now I should have been sending for them to come and live with me. I wonder if Natalia has told them what really happened to me. What she did.

Sasha was going to be a chef. She was the top student on her cookery course. She told me about all the dishes she has created, and it almost made me hungry to taste them. Almost.

As the afternoon wore on she told me about another girl she heard of who escaped. My ears pricked up, but I kept my eyes closed and gave nothing away. This girl was from Romania and worked in a brothel in Spain. One day the brothel was raided by the police and the girl was arrested with all the others and taken into custody. The girl did not tell the police what had happened to her because of threats by her pimp, who told her he would kill her family if she revealed what was really going on. It sounded familiar to me. Sasha said the police even let her pimp visit her in prison, where he repeated his threats to her. The girl did not feel safe enough to explain to the authorities that she had been trafficked, and when the Spanish immigration sent her back to Romania, her pimp found her and took her back again.

Maybe I should give up hope.

Day 27

I have some good news! I got a glimpse of a new girl who arrived here yesterday. She is from Moldova and lived in the next village to mine. Her name is Christina, and we went to school together. I want to ask her if she has news about my mother and Liliana but she is locked in her room. I remember it well. I know what will have happened to her to get her to comply.

I want to break her door down and hug her, and tell her everything will be all right, but that would make me a liar. I am disgusted with myself that I am happy she is here for my own selfish reasons. What kind of person am I becoming?

I am so excited to talk to her that I fidget on my bed and cannot keep still. I will have to wait until they let her out, though.

Please let my family be OK.

Day 30

The doctor has been again. My urine infection has gone and he said I am OK to work now. How would he know? How can any of us girls be OK to work? Doesn't he know that it is not just the physical side of it, but the mental side, too?

That was just the first bad news I had today.

When the doctor left I visited Christina in her room. Her door is now unlocked, but she is in a bad way. She cannot talk because the Rapist almost strangled her to death. There are bruises around her neck and she just makes scared, soft whimpers, like a wounded animal. I feel her pain.

The doctor must earn a fortune in this house.

I sat on the bed next to her, stroking her hair, which seemed to calm her down. I get the feeling she wants to tell me something important. Maybe it will make this place more bearable to have someone else here from home. I know it works that way for me.

I feel so much anger. It is bubbling away under the surface and threatening to explode. Anger for myself, for Christina, for Sasha and all the other girls. Anger towards everyone who is involved in this.

I stayed with her for an hour, until Angelina told me to get ready for the men. And, of course, I said nothing. I did not explode. I did not scream or lash out or cry. I did what I am told because it must be that way.

Day 32

The days and nights are all the same. If I did not keep my diary, I would not know what day it was as they all blend into one nightmare. I truly want to die, but every time I have this thought I see my baby's face.

Liliana keeps me alive.

I am anxious for news of her and my mother, but Christina still cannot talk. Part of me feels angry with Christina for this, and then a horrible guilt twists my stomach. It is not her fault she cannot tell me what I want to know.

Day 34

My mother is dead and Liliana has been sent to an orphanage.

I wish I did not know. I wish Christina still could not talk. I can hardly see the pages on my diary through my tears.

Christina said my mother had a heart attack about a week after I left. Liliana stayed with a neighbour, until the authorities came and took her away to who knows where.

They are gone, and I never got to say goodbye.

For hours I have sat in my room on the floor with my arms wrapped around me for comfort. My eyes are puffy and red, and Angelina will not be happy when she sees the state of me.

My mother has always been there to comfort me throughout my life. We did not have much money, it is true, but I never lacked any love or warmth. She was my rock. She told me I was special; that I could do whatever I wanted to in life.

Part of me hates her because she was wrong about that, and part of me hates her for leaving me. It is a stupid idea. Ridiculous, I know. How can I hate my mother?

I used to pour my heart out to her. I used to tell her everything. I am not sure I will be able to do that with anybody else. I do not think I could. All my dreams and hopes have disappeared with her.

And Liliana…

Is she safe? Are they hurting her in the orphanage? Is she getting enough to eat? Is she warm, or shivering with cold? Does she have clean clothes? Is Ivan with her? Is she hurt? Will she be kidnapped? Sold?

I have to find her.

I picture her, sitting on a dirty bed in a big, horrible dormitory with other small children who do not speak. She is staring at the floor with her huge dark eyes, sucking her thumb and wondering where her mummy and grandma have gone. Wondering why they have deserted her.

Oh, Liliana, I am here. I love you more than life itself, baby.

My heart feels like it has been ripped from my body, stamped on a million times, then pushed back in so I can carry on hurting. My stomach is on fire with uncontrollable flames of anger. The injustice of this world makes me sick. This is not fair. What have I done to deserve this?

I am empty inside. A horrible, dark, loneliness is crushing me from within.

Liliana.

How can I get to my baby from here?

I have an idea that has been tumbling around in my head since the policemen came. I do not know if I can do it. I do not know if it will work, but I have to try. I have to find Liliana.

Day 35

I feel like I am in a dark pit, trying to claw my way out. Pain, pain, pain in my soul that will never go away.

I cannot stand waiting for the policemen to arrive, and yet they are my only hope. Will they come tonight? I never thought I would long for one of the men to come and see me.

The minutes of the day tick by until it has been a whole hour. I do not know how, but I get through to the next hour, and then the next. Hoping. Waiting for my opportunity.

I have no energy, and I eat only because when the time comes I need to be ready. Food tastes of nothing. It is abrasive, and it is all I can do to swallow without choking.

Part of me is dead, too.

Day 37

I have made a very big mistake and I cannot change it. Now my situation is far worse.

Last night, when the policemen came, I acted willing, compliant. I wanted one of them to choose me. Inside I cringed as I draped my arms around them and flirted as if I wanted them.

Flirted! To me that word implies that I am free to do as I choose.

One of the younger policemen I had not seen before could not resist me. It was easy to get him into my bedroom. I was playing a game. Sexy, teasing. But nearby, in the corner of the room was my bag, ready and waiting.

I undressed him slowly as he licked his lips at the anticipation of what was to come.

I unbuttoned his shirt and threw it on the nearby chair.

It was easy to undo his belt with his gun and handcuffs on it and drape it over a nearby chair.

For once, I was in charge.

He let me handcuff his arms to the metal bedpost as I undid his trousers, hinting at what was to come – something kinky.

All the time I was thinking about getting to Liliana.

I knew I would not have much time. I had to use it wisely.

I blindfolded him with a black scarf and told him I had a surprise for him. He had to be patient and wait a few more minutes. And as I grabbed his gun and disappeared into my bathroom, I hurriedly pulled on jeans, a T-shirt, and some flat shoes.

I slipped out of my bedroom and locked the door from the outside. The corridor was clear as I rushed along and down the stairs with the gun in my hand.

I knew the Rapist would be in the kitchen playing cards with the other guards. I had to try and make it through the lounge to the front door before they knew what was happening. I prayed that I would make it out of there.

As I rushed through the lounge there were two girls in there, chatting. They looked up with surprise as I sped past them, grabbed the handle of the front door and turned it.

It clicked open.

Never had a sound filled me with such joy.

I stumbled into the night, running as fast as my legs would go before they realized what had happened.

The dark night sped past me as I travelled through unfamiliar streets. It was probably about five in the morning. I did not know where I was going, just that I had to get as far away as possible.

I kept expecting to feel a hand grabbing my shoulder and pulling me back so I did not dare look behind me or slow down.

I ran past bars and shops and houses and apartments until my chest hurt and I could no longer breathe. I passed men in the street who turned their heads and stared at me but I did not stop. What if they were friends of these people?

I found an alleyway behind a building and crouched in the dark shadows. I wiped my fingerprints off the gun with my T-shirt and threw it behind a pile of rotting rubbish. My plan was to wait there until I caught my breath, then somehow find the Moldovan Embassy. I would get home.

As my breath finally slowed down it hit me what had happened and I started shaking uncontrollably.

My T-shirt was soaked in sweat and my jeans clung to my legs. One of my shoes had come off as I was running, and it was only then that I noticed blood coming from cuts on the sole of my foot.

I had escaped, but what would they do now? Would they try and find me? How could they find me in this big city? Would they try and find Liliana? Surely they would not be able to steal her from the orphanage. There would be adults there all the time to supervise the children.

I did not know how to find the Embassy or Consulate. I had no money for a bus. Would a stranger help me?

I took deep breaths, gulping for oxygen to calm me, and walked tentatively back to the street, looking up and down. I needed to find a woman or a couple who would help me. There was a bar a little further down. Maybe there would be someone in there.

No one in the bar spoke English. They gave me odd looks and shrugged their shoulders at me. I must have looked dishevelled and strange to them.

I walked on further down the road to a small shop. There was a woman just opening up and stacking newspapers outside.

At last someone who might help me.

I tried to explain I wanted to get to the Embassy but she could not understand what I was saying.

As I stumbled further down the street a taxi driver called out to me.

'I have no money,' I cried. 'But I need to get to the Moldovan Embassy. Can you help me?' I pleaded with him.

I did not want to get inside a vehicle with this man, but what else could I do?

'No money, no taxi,' he said, turning back to his newspaper.

'Can you give me directions, then?' I wailed.

With much reluctance, he put down his paper. 'There is no Embassy,' he said, 'only a Consulate.' He gave me directions and told me it was not far.

I clutched my chest with relief and hurried off down the road.

The sun was just coming up as I saw the Consulate building in front of me, and for the first time since I had escaped, I allowed a huge smile to creep across my face. I did not think it would be open yet, but I planned on waiting somewhere close by where I could hide until it was.

In my mind, I was already playing with my daughter again. I was tickling her feet as she giggled uncontrollably. I was reading her a bedtime story and tucking her blanket in tight. I was walking hand in hand with her through the market.

I was so lost in my daydreams that I did not hear a car slowing to a halt behind me. I did not hear the footsteps or see the shadow on the pavement looming towards me until it was too late. The Rapist grabbed me and shoved me, kicking and screaming, into the car.

I took a risk to escape and it did not work. That decision will always haunt me.

Day 38

The Rapist enjoyed beating me before he raped me. This time he did not touch my face, though. They are going to sell me to someone else and they want me to look pretty. It did not stop him kicking, punching, and slapping me everywhere else. When he finally pulled himself out of me, he said, 'Do you want your daughter alive or dead? Try anything again and I will slit her throat.' Then he leered at me, baring his dirty teeth. 'I think I will rape her, too, before I kill her.'

I am a troublemaker, they said. They do not need the hassle. Angelina later told me they had thought about killing me, but I am more valuable alive. For now. She seemed to enjoy telling me that Liliana is living with Natalia now. She said the orphanages are poor, and if they can offload a child, they will.

Before Angelina left she locked me in my room, and as punishment she took the few things I have collected in my time here. I do not care that she has taken my magazines and playing cards that Sasha gave me. The only thing I can think about is Liliana with Natalia. What is Natalia telling her about me? Has she told Liliana I do not love her anymore? That I do not want her? Will she sell my sweet baby to traffickers? Will she feed her and keep her warm? I think about the things the Rapist said. Would he carry out his threats against

Liliana? I cannot bear all the thoughts and fears screaming in my head. I can take the external torture, but the internal torture is far, far worse.

I want to kill them all. I fantasize about how I would do it. Shooting them would be too good. I want to make them hurt and cause them agony. A knife, perhaps, or an iron bar – something that will make them suffer the way they make me and the other girls suffer.

But there is nothing I can do now.

Last year Liliana wanted me to buy her a watch. She saw mine and became obsessed with it, as only children can. "Why do you wear it?"; "What is it for?"; "Is everyone's time in the whole world the same?"; "Who decides what the time is?" On and on she asked questions until I let her wear it.

A watch is useless in here. I do not need a watch to sit and wait, and pass seconds that feel like a whole lifetime has gone by. I do not need a watch to know that now it will take me an infinite time to gain the trust of my new owners. And without their trust I cannot dare to dream of getting back to Liliana. They will be watching every move I make.

So I will behave myself and fool them into thinking I am the best sex slave they have ever had. And one day there will be another chance. I have to believe that or else I will go insane.

Day 40

I am trying to remember the last thing I ever bought. Groceries? Wool for my mother to knit us winter jumpers? A plastic hair clip for Liliana? Milk? I cannot remember.

The last thing Paul Robb bought is me.

He is my new owner, and Angelina said he will be coming to get me today. I will be going to one of his saunas or brothels in England.

It is strange for me to admit this, but I am going to miss it here. At least here the men must wear condoms and I have my own bathroom. The house is nice and clean, and I can see the sunlight through the windows, even though I can never feel it on my face.

I think of the stories Sasha and the other girls have told me, and I fear what my new prison will be like.

I have a feeling it will be worse. Much worse.

Day 45

When Stefan used to tell me I was beautiful, it always lit me up inside. He did it a lot. I would catch him watching me with a proud smile on his face at odd moments in the day. Every night in each other's arms, before we drifted off to sleep, he would tell me I was the most gorgeous girl in the world.

When Paul looked at me and said I was beautiful it made me cringe. He is not saying it to a lover or a wife. He is looking at me like an object. Something that will make him money.

I tried to engage my new owner in conversation on our drive from Italy to England, pretending to be friendly and chatty, but he would tell me to shut up. In the deafening silence I could hear my life ticking away.

I only know three things about my new circumstances: 1) I now have a false British passport – I saw it as he handed it to the guards at each border; 2) He will kill Liliana if I do not do as he says; 3) He is no better than the Rapist.

It has taken three days to arrive in England. As we sped through villages and towns, I wondered how many other women like me were out there. The more miles we drove, the more a heavy pressure settled in my chest, as if squeezing the life out of me.

He has already asserted his authority over me with rough sex and threats during the two nights we stayed in small motels on the journey. But I want him to trust me, so I pretend I am enthusiastic, even though I want to batter him until his brains explode. I have become a learned student in acting, and I will use this skill well.

My new cell is in an apartment that is a massage parlour somewhere in London. This is not the picture I had in my head of the city when my father told me it was a great place to start a new life. It is in a shabby and busy street, and I think the men will be worse here than before. A big, rusting sign hangs outside, advertising *P's Massage Parlour* for all the world to see. Every single person who walks or drives past this place can see it, yet no one does anything. They are trafficking girls under everyone's noses, but we are invisible.

My room has shaggy pink carpet and pink wallpaper with frayed edges. It stinks from years of neglect and proper cleaning. The double bed is sagging and worn and it squeaks with the slightest movement. There are no bars on the window, but I am four storeys up and would probably kill myself if I jumped. Maybe that would be a good thing.

I have no bathroom in my cell. There is a shared bathroom that the girls must use, with mould around the edges and leaking taps that have left greenish-brown stains on the white surface. There is a cracked mirror on the wall and my reflection sums me up perfectly.

  Broken.

Day 49

I studied myself in the mirror and realized I have lost more weight. My hips bones and ribs stick out more, my eyes are sunken in my skull, and my stomach is concave. They give us food in small amounts, and if we want more we have to ask for it. I never ask. I do not want to eat, and I do not want to give them the satisfaction.

None of the girls here talk about themselves like Sasha did. We are all nervous in case anything we say gets back to our captors. There could be one who is willing to pass on anything we say for the promise of better treatment.

The days and nights are all the same again. The men come – drunk, dirty, smelly. Sometimes they are violent and they are thrown out, but nothing bad happens to them. They are filthy pigs, but I am the perfect whore.

Paul is pleased with me. He said if I am good, I can visit the rich men he provides girls for. Anything is better than the men here.

Liliana fills every waking thought, and she is with me permanently in my dreams. She is the only thing that gets me through this.

Just before I was trafficked I made her a pretend telephone. We could not afford a real one, so I tied two plastic cups to the ends of a long piece of string. She would go in one room and put the cup to her ear to see if she could hear me talking, then make me do the same.

I talk to her all the time in my head now, hoping somehow that she can telepathically hear me. Liliana is at the mercy of Natalia, Andrei, the Rapist, Paul, and many others I have never even met. Her life used to be in my hands. Now it is in theirs alone.

Day 53

Yesterday I was allowed outside. Not to shop or sightsee or visit a friend, like most people take for granted, but to visit a rich customer.

Paul has an expensive apartment in London that he keeps for his big-payers, and he drove me there in his shiny, luxurious car. He calls this "The Millionaires' Club."

He told me the man had booked me for the whole night. Tomorrow I must call Paul and he will pick me up.

The apartment was like something in a magazine – modern with big windows and minimal furniture. It was spotlessly clean with sparkling chrome and glass, and the area of London looks expensive and well-cared for. The complete opposite of the massage parlour. It is on the fifteenth floor of the building, and I could look down to the huge river below. For a moment I wondered what it would feel like to run through the glass and dive into the water. Into oblivion.

I had my bag with me and my "sexy" clothes inside. Paul told me I must look beautiful for this man, so I brushed my hair until it shone like ebony and you cannot tell that it is coming out by the handful. I applied my make-up to hide the dark circles under my eyes and my pale skin. My skin smelled of vanilla from the perfume Paul gave me to wear so this man will not smell the mould from the bathroom I shower in. From the way Paul talked, I knew this man was an important customer and I had to make a special effort.

This was the first time I had been outside on my own since I was trafficked, and Paul let me know in no uncertain terms what will happen to Liliana if I did something stupid.

When Paul left, I went into one of the bedrooms to get ready for this man. I was told he likes being tied up and whipped. Then he likes to act out a rape fantasy.

He arrived in an expensive-looking suit. He has light brown hair and pale blue eyes. He is probably about forty-eight years old. He did not waste time ordering me to do this and that: Undress him while I am naked, except for knee-length leather boots. Tie him to the bed by his legs and arms. Whip him lightly and shout filthy things to him. Then, when he was ready, he ordered me to untie him.

Next, it was my turn to be whipped. Only he enjoyed doing it harder. Not enough to rip my skin, but I have sore, red welts there now. He liked to handcuff my wrists and ankles to the bed and strangle me as he raped me. This went on throughout the night. Time and again.

Today I cannot talk. There are bruises around my throat and marks on my body. At 8 a.m. the man got dressed, and as he did up his cufflinks he stared at me. He did not really see me; I am just a thing to him.

'I like you,' he said, nodding his approval. 'Paul made a good choice. I'll see you the same time next week.' He handed me a one hundred pound tip.

I cannot keep it, of course. I have to give it to Paul so he knows he can trust me. Paul was very pleased with me. He showed his pleasure by ripping my clothes off as soon as I got into my bedroom at the massage parlour. He had a huge, ugly grin on his face as he saw the bruises and marks across my white skin.

'Oh, yeah, baby. He likes you. You're going to make me a fortune,' Paul said before throwing me on the bed and raping me.

I squeezed my eyes closed and prayed for this nightmare to end.

Day 54

Yesterday was my initiation into "The Millionaires' Club." Paul told me the Strangler was so pleased with me, he was going to use me regularly at the apartment for the other rich men. Tonight Paul will take me to that place again, and I will spend hours making myself look pretty for them.

Day 56

Every night I have the same nightmare. I am trapped in a coffin, buried alive underground. I can actually smell the peat in the ground and feel the cold earth permeate my bones so I am shivering. There are insects crawling over my skin. Cockroaches and spiders. Then the rats come later and gnaw on my skin.

When I bang on the wooden lid, trying to tell someone I am trapped, I hear my mother calling me.

'Elena, where are you?' she cries.

And even though I am just below her, a few feet underground, she cannot hear me.

My nails scrape against the sides of the coffin, and I kick it with my feet, but I cannot get out.

After I wake up in a cold sweat, my skin itches uncontrollably and I cannot get back to sleep.

Day 57

I have a new customer who did not want to have sex with me. I do not know if this is some kind of loyalty test that Paul has conjured up so he knows he can trust me, or if it is something else.

The man is called Jamie. He was my first customer tonight at the massage parlour, and I could tell he was nervous. He would hardly look me in the eye. He reminds me of Stefan in some small way. Not the way he looks, but how he holds himself. It seems like there is something gentle about him.

I asked him what he wanted and he did not seem to understand me.

'What would you like me to do for you?' I said to him.

His eyebrows furrowed slightly, as if I was trying to trick him. 'Look…er…I've never done this kind of thing before. I just want to talk,' he said.

'Talk?' I repeated. I thought I had misheard him because this has never happened before.

'Yes. And I want to hold you,' he said.

So we laid on the bed together and he held me in his arms, chest to chest, his chin resting on the top of my head. He told me how his wife died a year ago from a sudden brain haemorrhage. It has been hard for him, coping without her. He misses her in his arms at night, and I know how he feels, because he makes me think about Stefan again. He said he has been lonely, and he needs to get comfort from someone.

So I stroked his back gently and let him talk about her, trying to give him all the comfort I could. It is much better than being raped.

Day 59

I spend a lot of time at Paul's Millionaires' Club apartment now.

One of the men likes two girls at a time. One of them wants me to dress like a school girl. One of them likes me to wear a certain perfume. One of them likes me to whip him.

Most of the rich men treat me better than the men in the massage parlour, and I am grateful for that. The only exception is the Strangler.

Day 65

Jamie came to see me again. This time he paid for three hours of my time, but he still did not want sex. It was the same as before, lying on the bed in each other's arms as he talked about his wife.

It made me think of Stefan when he told me they were childhood sweethearts. After going their separate ways to university, they lost touch with each other, but met up by chance a few years later and got married when they were twenty-five. Although they had no children, they had been trying for a baby for the last four years. One day she was there, the next she was gone. Her life disappeared in a puff of smoke. I can relate to that.

I discovered he is thirty-five years old and has a cat called Whiskers.

For the first time ever, a man has asked me why I do this job. I get the feeling he thinks this is my choice. Do people really think every prostitute turns to this life because they are nymphomaniacs? Because it is their number one career choice? Do they honestly think some women and girls aspire to be a sex slave whore like they aspire to be a pop star? I wish the world would wake up.

I was aching to tell him the truth, but I did not dare. What if it is a trap? So I steered the conversation back to him as the minutes of the night slipped by.

Day 82

My life drags on, but now there is some kind of routine. Five days a week I am used by "The Millionaires' Club", and three times a week Jamie comes to see me.

Jamie reads the paper to me, or stories, or poems. I like poems the best – there is something magical about them. Today I saw a picture of the Strangler in the paper, and asked Jamie to read the story about him. He is the Foreign Minister. Ironic, isn't it? I sat there wondering what makes a man in that position do this. I used to think it was just poor countries that fed corruption and deceit, but now I think it has poisoned the veins of the whole world. I hide my surprise about this politician by asking Jamie to play one of the card games he has taught me. We played Rummy and Whist on the bed, and he is always very gracious when I beat him.

Somehow, in the midst of all this, he has taught me to laugh again.

We talk about a lot of things, but the only thing I do not tell him is how I got here and who I am. Somehow I feel an invisible bond with him – a closeness that I cannot explain. I look forward to his visits because he only seems to want female companionship. If I am honest, I feel something like excitement when I see him. He does not want to use and abuse me like the others, and he is the only man since I was taken who treats me like a real person. I would like to think I can trust him now, but I do not know for certain, so I still say nothing about being trafficked.

Day 86

When we were dating, Stefan came to visit with a bunch of wild flowers for me. Pinks and yellows and blues lit up my bare windowsill, and the smell was incredible. I arranged them neatly in a tin cup, and every time I walked past them I would take a sniff and admire their simple beauty. It was the first present he ever gave me, and whenever he could find pretty flowers after that he would always pick them for me.

Today, when Jamie brought me a bunch of flowers and awkwardly presented them to me, I cried. All the pent up hurt, pain, and anger suddenly spewed out of me, and when I started, I could not stop. He gently held me in his arms, rocking me like my mother used to do when I was a child, as he made shushing sounds.

I wondered why something as simple as a flower had triggered such emotion from me when I had been trying so hard to keep it all inside, and then I realized it was not the flowers at all. It was the gesture.

That is when I knew I should trust this man, and so I finally opened up and told him everything that had happened to me. He was silent while I talked, but I knew from the look on his face he was horrified.

He told me he assumed I was a willing participant who enjoyed sex – that I chose this profession. He thought I was earning most of the money the massage parlour charged, which is £50 for half an hour, so maybe I was attracted by the lure of good money. He thought that I did it because maybe I had a drug habit, or was unable to get a regular job for some reason. He thought I was in control of my life.

He had so many false ideas about me and how I came to be here that when he realized, he cried right along with me.

'I have a friend who is a policeman,' he told me before his time was up. 'I will speak to him as soon as I get home.'

'You will have to be very careful about how you go about things,' I pleaded with him. 'They will kill my daughter if they find out I told anyone.'

He hugged me tight. 'Don't worry, it will be discreet. I *will* get you out of here.'

And I believed him.

Day 87

I finally have hope, and it is like someone has injected some magical substance into my veins that fills me with excitement. I am buzzing with happiness, and I cannot wait to see Jamie and discover how soon the police will take me out of here.

I think back to the policemen in Italy and hope they are not the same here. I push those thoughts to the back of my mind and wait for Jamie to arrive.

When Jamie came to see me today, he was awkward again. He told me he feels tremendous guilt for assuming things about me, but I do not care about that.

I took his hand and rushed him to sit on the bed and tell me everything that happened with his friend.

'He is a sergeant in one of the Criminal Investigation Departments in the Metropolitan Police. I told him everything you told me and he is passing it onto the Clubs and Vice Unit. He thinks it will only be a matter of days until they arrange a search warrant and raid the premises.'

I clutched his arm. 'But what about Liliana?'

He took both my hands in his, gripping them tightly. 'These people won't know you had anything to do with this. My friend said the police will take all the girls here into custody when they arrive. You'll be protected then, and after that, we can get the Moldovan Embassy to check on Liliana and keep her safe.' He gave me a reassuring smile.

Day 88

The politician's demands are the same, but I know it will soon be over so I can put up with him and all the other men.

My main concern is Liliana. Will Paul and the others somehow find out I was involved in this and carry out retribution against her? I twist all the possible scenarios around in my brain on an endless loop.

I do not think they will find out, but if I am arrested, how do I get to Liliana? I pray that the Embassy can make enquiries and find out if she is still with Natalia in our village. I daydream about them whisking her away to safety. Until she is safe, I cannot speak out loud and tell the truth about what happened to me.

I pace the floor when I am not working and wait for news from Jamie.

When he arrived, he said he had made enquiries with the Embassy, and they would not look into Liliana's whereabouts until they heard the story from me and verified it. I need to go to the Embassy and tell them everything personally. It seems ludicrous to me. I would go there if I could. No amount of persuasion by Jamie would make them change their minds. Until they have a relative of Liliana making an official complaint to them or a court order, they will do nothing, so I must wait for the police to take me to safety before I tell them.

Our time together was short. Jamie only stayed half an hour because he does not want to be here when the police arrive.

Day 89

There was no search warrant, no teams of policemen. Only two officers arrived in uniform at eleven o'clock in the morning, when all the customers had gone.

Paul was here when they came, and the police lined all the girls up in the reception area. They explained they had an anonymous tipoff that some of the girls were being kept here against their will, and asked all of us to confirm that we were here by our own choice.

I wanted to die inside. I wanted to scream, "YES," from the top of my lungs. I wanted to clutch their legs and beg them to take me away. But Paul was in the very room. What could we say?

Paul was purple with rage when they left, and all of the girls were subject to kicks and bodily punches. He went lightly on me because he does not want the Millionaires' Club men to ask too many questions.

But I am the most angry, and I do not have the satisfaction of venting my anger. I can only turn it inward and fester.

I have had enough of being an actress trapped in a victim's body.

I tug at my hair until clumps of it are coming out at the roots. I bite the inside of my cheeks until I taste metallic blood. I gnaw on my fingernails until they hurt.

The police know this is a brothel so why don't they shut it down? Isn't it illegal here? They do not care.

I feel defeated. Is there no end to this torment?

Day 97

Still the police do nothing. Jamie has been to see his friend many times, but the answer is the same: They cannot do anything without evidence. Jamie cannot make a statement to them about the things I said until Liliana is safe, so they have no evidence. I am in a catch 22 situation.

Day 98

When I was a little girl, I would get so excited before my birthday. I looked forward to it for months, asking my mother all the time how many more days I would have to wait until I was another year older. It was not just the presents I anticipated with happiness – they were always small and inexpensive. No, the thing I looked forward to most was being a big girl. Because when I was a big girl, my father told me I could do anything and go anywhere I wanted; the world was full of opportunities that way. At that age I wanted to be a ballerina or a vet.

Now I am a big girl and I look forward to being raped by millionaires. It is twisted and sick, isn't it? I look forward to seeing those men because they are cleaner than most of the men at the massage parlour. It is the one time when I can go outside and smell the fresh air. I can see the river, the stars, the sparkling lights of the city. Somehow, it gives me hope. There is a whole world that exists outside of the massage parlour, and I have a feeling somewhere in that world is an opportunity for me to get my real life back.

Day 99

Yesterday night the politician played out his sick games with me again.

And, as he thrust inside me and squeezed my throat with more vigour than before, a plan formed in my head, and I thought of two things before I lost consciousness...

If I am dead, no one can help Liliana.

I am tired of waiting.

Day 100

I need Jamie's help to carry out my plan. Since Paul believes I am the perfect, compliant slave, he never thinks to search me before my torture with the politician in the confines of "The Millionaires' Club."

It was easy for Jamie to smuggle in a small video recorder when he came to see me. I have no idea how to use such modern and complicated technology, and for a minute I was scared that I could not do this. But Jamie came to my rescue, patiently showing me how to work the buttons and giving me constant reassurance. For three hours I took videos of him and then deleted them again – over and over until I could work the camera blindfolded. By the time he left I was feeling more confident.

Please let this work.

Day 101

Paul suspected nothing as he dropped me off at the apartment. It did not take me long to find the perfect hiding place for the video camera on a shelf opposite the bed.

This was my only chance, and the enormity of it gave me butterflies. I wanted to be sick, but instead I gulped cold glasses of water to settle my stomach until the politician arrived.

I checked the digital clock by the bed for the millionth time, waiting for the agonizingly slow minutes to pass until he arrived.

When he finally rang the doorbell, I double-checked the position of the camera with shaky fingers and set it to record.

I have had a long time to perfect my acting skills. Now they will be put to the test.

I did not dare watch the video when I arrived back at the massage parlour. Instead, I hid it beneath a loose floorboard under the carpet in my bedroom. I pray that I managed to work it properly, and that every sick thing he did to me is captured clearly.

Day 106

The wheels of justice turn quickly when you have the weight of blackmail behind you. So much has happened that thoughts are jumbling around in my head all at once. I will try and start at the beginning.

After Jamie smuggled the video out of the massage parlour, his policeman friend managed to arrange a private meeting between Jamie and the politician.

From what I understand, the politician used his contacts to order a raid on the massage parlour. Everyone was taken into custody at the police station. I was kept in a cell on my own for four hours before a lady from the Moldovan Embassy called Katya came to see me.

Through the deluge of tears, I told her my story, and that I needed Liliana to be safe before I could make a statement about what had happened to me. I was scared that she would not believe me. To some people, the story would seem so unreal that it must be complete fabrication. But she did believe me. I saw the tears in her eyes, too, as she took notes, comforted me, and tried to keep her own composure. I did not mention the politician, but she said the police have been instructed by powers "high up" to assist me in every way they can.

Katya told me that the Foreign Minister had somehow heard of my story and was pulling strings with the Immigration Department in Britain and the government in Moldova. They would be searching for Liliana immediately.

She also told me the British Immigration Department were issuing a temporary visa for me. If I was willing to give evidence against the traffickers, they would grant a full visa so I could stay here.

'It is very unusual,' Katya said, 'that the Foreign Office and Immigration Department should go to this much trouble. I have never seen it happen like this before.'

I just nodded at her, as if I were unaware of this, and asked her more questions.

I had been in the police cell for twenty-four hours when Katya came to see me again.

'We have found Liliana,' she said breathlessly, enveloping me in a hug as a cry like a wounded animal escaped from my lips and I collapsed to the floor.

When I could get my breath back, she told me that Liliana had not been living with Natalia. That was a lie by the Rapist and the others to coerce me. Liliana had been in a state orphanage all this time. Katya told me that since I could not leave the country at the moment, under the circumstances, the British government would be willing to allow Liliana to be flown here to me and would even pay for the airfare.

I was kept in the police station for another twenty-four hours for my own safety. I was told that Paul was still in custody, but none of the other girls had spoken out about being trafficked. They would be relying on my statement to prosecute him.

The enormous weight of this settled on my chest and I could not breathe, but one thought kept me strong. I was determined that he and the others should never be able to do this to anyone else.

For the first time in 106 days, I was in control.

Jamie was allowed to visit me and again I broke down. All the aggression, hurt, tears, anger, degradation, shame...it all came to the surface and exploded. Just like before, he held me in his arms and rocked me, without asking for anything from me in return.

It is strange, but part of me feels love towards him for that. I did not think that I would ever be able to feel anything for anybody again. I thought I would be emotionally dead, but over this time we have built up a friendship that is beyond explainable. I trust this man. I believe he is a good person, and part of me loves him for not giving up on me. Without him, I would still be in that place. I owe him my life.

And Jamie's help never seems to end. He offered to fly to Moldova to bring Liliana back with him on the plane so she will not be alone and frightened. He sat with me while I wrote a letter to her to read on her journey so she knows she is coming to see me and will not be scared.

For a third day, they kept me in custody for my protection, but I did not mind. It was still a cell, but it was a halfway home to freedom.

I was not released from custody until Liliana was on the aeroplane to Britain. The thought of seeing her again made my throat constrict. Katya had been told by the Maldovan authorities that they had accompanied Liliana and Jamie onto the plane and it had taken off on time.

I was finally released under a police escort, and along with Katya, we travelled to Gatwick Airport with tense excitement.

I craned my neck at the arrivals area, waiting for the slightest glimpse of my beautiful Liliana. Suddenly she appeared, her little hand held tight in Jamie's. And then she was running towards me.

I picked up my baby girl and held her tight. Squeezing her to me as the tears snaked down my cheeks and landed on her hair. She wrapped her legs around my waist and rested her head on my shoulder.

'Where have you been, Mummy?' she said.

Words that broke my heart.

Day 107

My new home is in a hostel for vulnerable women. There are many women like me here. I know; I can see it in their eyes. Although everyone is friendly, most of them find it too raw to talk about how they came to be here. We are all in the same situation: adjusting our lives in the hope we can mend and become whole again.

Children adapt to things quickly. I wish I could, too. Liliana has not mentioned the orphanage, and I do not want to pressure her to talk about it in case it makes her scared or unhappy. She hugs Ivan close to her chest and follows me everywhere I go, chatting constantly like she has been deprived of speech since I last saw her. She is inquisitive about this new country...

'Will I meet the Queen?'; 'Why are we here?'; 'Who are the other ladies here?'; 'Why is your hair falling out?'

She seems happy and contented just to be with me again, but she is sad when we talk about my mother.

I miss her and so does Liliana. I want to visit her grave and say goodbye properly, but I cannot go there. What if the Rapist and the others find me and take me back? I do not know if I can ever go back to Moldova. So instead, my mother will forever be alive in my heart and in my memories. Just like my father and Stefan.

Although the hostel is in a secret location, I do not go out alone. Paul is still in custody, but I worry that he could get someone to find us. This is what my life will be like from now on. I am free, but will I ever truly live as a free person?

I do not sleep well. Noises like the banging of a car door or shouting outside late at night frighten me. I wake up with my heart pounding, threatening to explode out of my chest. Liliana sleeps in my arms on the small bed we share. I do not have much, but it is enough.

We are together and that is all that matters.

Six Months Later

I am living one day at a time, but at least I *am* living.

Liliana and I now have a British visa to stay here, and I live in a small two-bedroom apartment with a security entrance. It has a balcony, overlooking a park. I love to stand on the safety of the balcony and stare at the outdoors. I relish the feeling of the sun on my cheeks as I take deep gulps of fresh air. It is little things like this I have come to appreciate.

I am still scared every day. I look over my shoulder all the time whenever I go out, and as one hand grips Liliana's tightly, the other is firmly pressed around a can of pepper spray in my pocket. I have nightmares every night. I am being chased and people are trying to kill me. When I wake up, it takes me a long time to get back to sleep, even though I feel the reassuring touch of the knife under my pillow. Although we have two bedrooms, Liliana and I both sleep in the same one, our arms wrapped around each other's, like how I used to sleep with Stefan. I do not want to let her go. She sleeps deep enough not to hear my nightmares, but she complains that I never let her out of my sight.

I have a job now as a volunteer. I work with other women who have been trafficked, and try to help them. I think it will aid my healing process, too. I remember my father's words every day. He whispers in my ear that I should do something special with my life in England. I think he would be proud of me.

I see Jamie several times a week. We take Liliana to the park or cinema, or just sit and chat. Liliana is in love with Whiskers. Jamie is my best friend and I treasure that friendship. Maybe one day it will become more, but I cannot think of that now. Little by little, second by second I am getting better. Over time I can only hope the internal and external scars will fade, although I know they will never disappear. I have been offered counselling but I do not want to talk about what happened with someone who can never truly understand what it is like. The best therapy for me is to try and help the others.

I now have hope in the future, and for that I must thank Jamie and Katya.

I still have a copy of the video and it is my security in this new world I am living in.

The trial will be starting soon. The lawyers have told me Paul will be sent to prison, and the Italian and Moldovan police are working in conjunction with the British police to prosecute the Rapist, Natalia, Andrei, Angelina and the rest of that gang. But what about the other traffickers in the world?

I am one of the lucky ones who managed to escape. There are thousands out there who have not.

A Note from the Author

About five years ago I watched a mini series about girls from Eastern Europe who'd been trafficked. It haunted me for a long time, and then gradually it faded from my mind and I got on with my life. Then a little while ago I was sitting in a doctor's surgery waiting for an appointment and picked up a magazine. Inside, was the story of one women who'd been trafficked. It made a chill run through me, and I realized that in those five years, I'd never heard anything in the media about it.

That got me thinking, and I started researching other victim's stories online. They were horrific, heart breaking, gut wrenching, and I knew this was a subject that, despite being such a global problem, a lot of people are unaware goes on. I really wanted to do something to raise awareness into the subject and Trafficked: The Diary of a Sex Slave was born.

Although the book is fictional, it's inspired by these victim's stories, and is a very sad global reality. In 2007 the US Department of State carried out a Trafficking in Persons report. The statistics shocked me to the core: 700,000-800,000 men, women and children trafficked across international borders each year, approximately 80% of which are women and girls, and up to 50% are minors. The figures will be a lot higher four years on.

And one of the truly scary things is, most people think it only affects third world countries, but it's going on right under your nose. The US Department of State estimated 14,500 to 17,500 foreign nationals are trafficked into the United States alone each year.

I wanted Trafficked to be gritty, hard hitting, and tear-jerking. And I wanted it to make people really stop and think about this subject. I chose to write it in the form of a diary so the reader really feels every emotion – the fear, beatings, horror, desperation, hope, and faith. I wanted you to experience the ordeal through the eyes of all the Elenas out there.

I'm donating 20 % of the royalties from the sale of this book to two leading UK based anti-trafficking charities. The donations will be paid monthly and split between The Poppy Project and Unseen UK. The more sales, the more donations can be made!

Trafficking Organizations:

http://www.sophiehayesfoundation.org/

http://www.stopthetraffik.org/language.aspx

http://www.acf.hhs.gov/trafficking/

http://www.humantrafficking.org/

http://www.eaves4women.co.uk/POPPY_Project/POPPY_Project.php

http://www.unseenuk.org/projects/support-services

http://www.gems-girls.org/about

http://www.endhumantraffickingnow.com/

About the Author

Sibel Hodge is an International Bestselling and Award Winning Author.

Her work has been shortlisted for the Harry Bowling Prize 2008, Highly Commended by the Yeovil Literary Prize 2009, Runner up in the Chapter One Promotions Novel Comp 2009, nominated Best Novel with Romantic Elements in 2010 by The Romance Reviews, and Winner of Best Children's Book by eFestival of Words 2013. Her novella *Trafficked: The Diary of a Sex Slave* has been listed as one of the Top 40 Books About Human Rights by Accredited Online Colleges.

For more information, please visit www.sibelhodge.com

Also by Sibel Hodge

Fiction:
Look Behind You
Butterfly
The See-Through Leopard
Fashion, Lies, and Murder (Amber Fox Mystery No 1)
Money, Lies, and Murder (Amber Fox Mystery No 2)
Voodoo, Lies, and Murder (Amber Fox Mystery No 3)
Chocolate, Lies, and Murder (Amber Fox Mystery No 4)
Fourteen Days Later
My Perfect Wedding
The Baby Trap
***How to Dump Your Boyfriend in the Men's Room (and
other short stories)***
It's a Catastrophe

Non Fiction:
A Gluten Free Taste of Turkey
A Gluten Free Soup Opera
Healing Meditations for Surviving Grief and Loss

Trafficked: The Diary of a Sex Slave
by
Sibel Hodge

Copyright © Sibel Hodge 2011

Made in the USA
Lexington, KY
24 June 2014